WOLFGANG AMADEUS

Concertos

For the Piano

Critically Revised, Fingered, and
the Orchestral Accompaniments
Arranged for a Second Piano

by FRANZ KULLAK

AND OTHERS

In D minor (Köchel 466) [F. Kullak] — Library Vol. 661
In C major (Köchel 467) [Bischoff] — Library Vol. 662
In E-flat major (Köchel 482) [Bischoff] — Library Vol. 663
In C minor (Köchel 491) [Bischoff] — Library Vol. 664
In D major (Köchel 537) [Rehberg] — Library Vol. 665
In A major (Köchel 488) [York] — Library Vol. 1584
In F major (Köchel 459) [Philipp] —Library Vol. 1701
In E-flat major (Köchel 271) [Philipp] — Library Vol. 1704
In B-flat major (Köchel 595) [Philipp] —Library Vol. 1721
In A major (Köchel 414) [Philipp] —Library Vol. 1731
In G major (Köchel 453) [Philipp] —Library Vol. 1734
→ In B-flat major (Köchel 450) [Philipp] —Library Vol. 1746

G. SCHIRMER, *Inc.*

Mozart completed this Concerto on March 15, 1784, in Vienna and performed it on the 17th. He reported to his father that "the hall was full to overflowing; and the new concerto I played won extraordinary applause".

The cadenzas in this edition are Mozart's own.

Concerto in B-flat Major

for Piano and Orchestra

[K. 450]

Edited by
Isidor Philipp

Wolfgang Amadeus Mozart
(1756-1791)

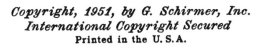

II
f
Ped.
ff
p

II
p
II
II
fp
cresc.
p
Ped. *
II
mf
f
Ped. *
II
simile

II
p
cresc.
A
p
I
f
p
leggero

I
II
cresc.
Ped.
f
B

I
II
p
I
II
Ped.
I
II
mf
p

I
II
p
cresc.
f
Ped.
C
dolce
tr

I
II
p
cresc.
fp
Ped.
Ped.

I
II
fp
Ped.
D
f
p

I
II
p
tr
Ped.
I
II
I
II

I
II
Ped.
E
cresc.
f

I
II
F
Ped.
f
p

I
II
I
II
cresc.
I
II
cresc.
tr
p
f
f

II
Ped.
p
G
mf
I

I
I
I
I
I
I
II
p
Ped.
*

H
leggero
p
Ped.
Ped.
Ped.

I
II
Ped.
f

I

II

I

II

I

II

I
II
cresc.
cresc.
f
f
Ped.
K
p

I
II
cresc.
Ped.
fp
L
f
p

I
II
p
tr
Ped.
Ped.
Ped.
Ped.
Ped.

I
II
Ped.
M
dolce
p
tr

I
II
p
leggero
Ped. *
simile

I
II
cresc.
cresc.
tr
N
p
Ped.
Ped.

O
I
II
f
f
Ped.
dim.
p
p

I
II
f
tr
fp

cresc.
Ped.
f
P
Cadenza
p
graceful

I
mf
p
cresc.
f
Ped.

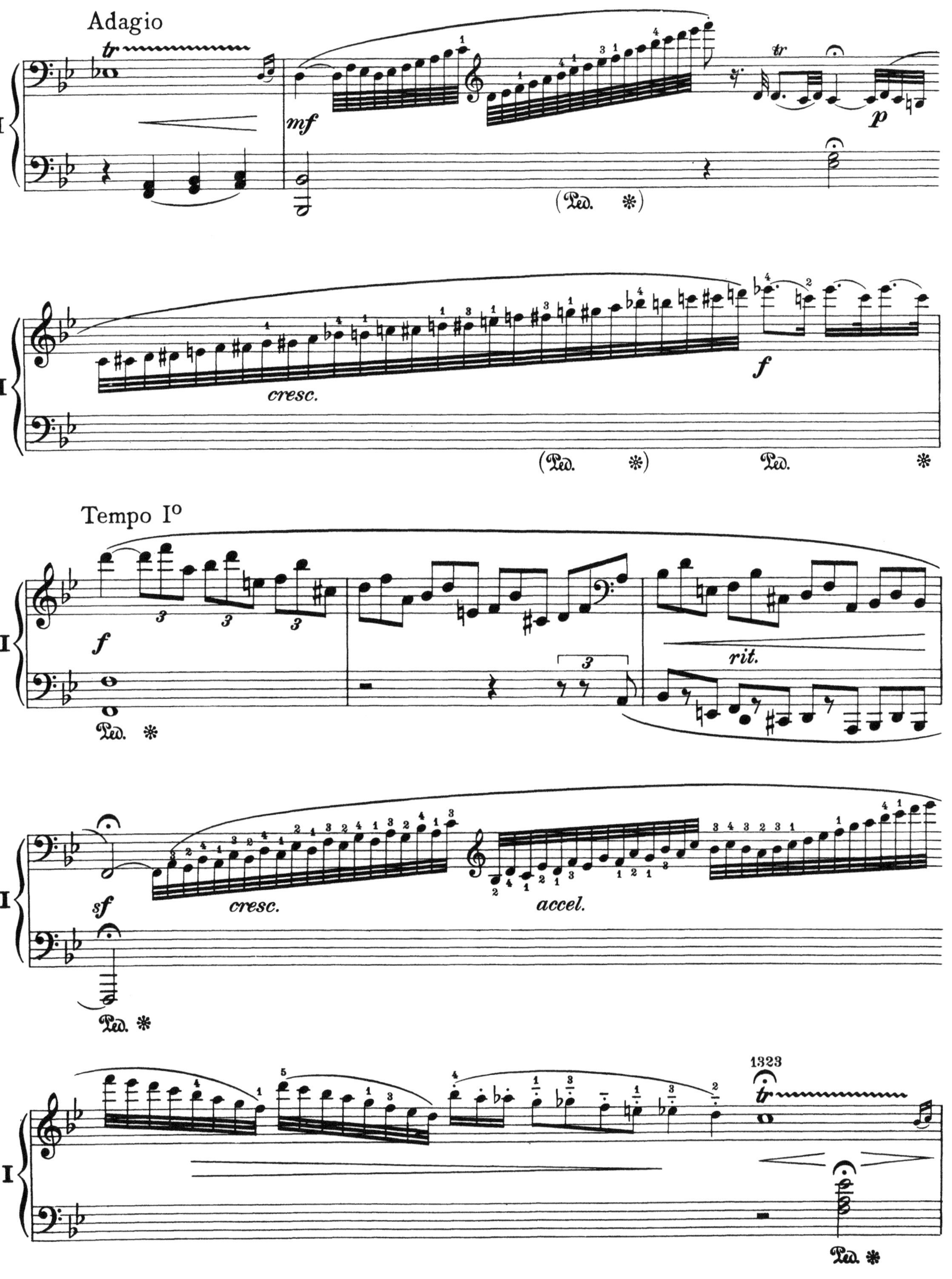

Adagio
tr
mf
(Ped. *)
p
cresc.
f
(Ped. *)
Ped. *
Tempo I°
f
Ped. *
rit.
sf
cresc.
accel.
Ped. *
1323
tr
Ped. *

I
II
f
tr
Ped.
simile
p
f
II
II
II
II

Andante ♪= 69
I
Andante ♪= 69
II
sempre p

I
II
I
II
A
I
II
p
p
p

I
II
f
mf
Ped.

I
II
f
B
p
Ped.
42474

I
II
p
tr
cresc.
p
C
pp
p

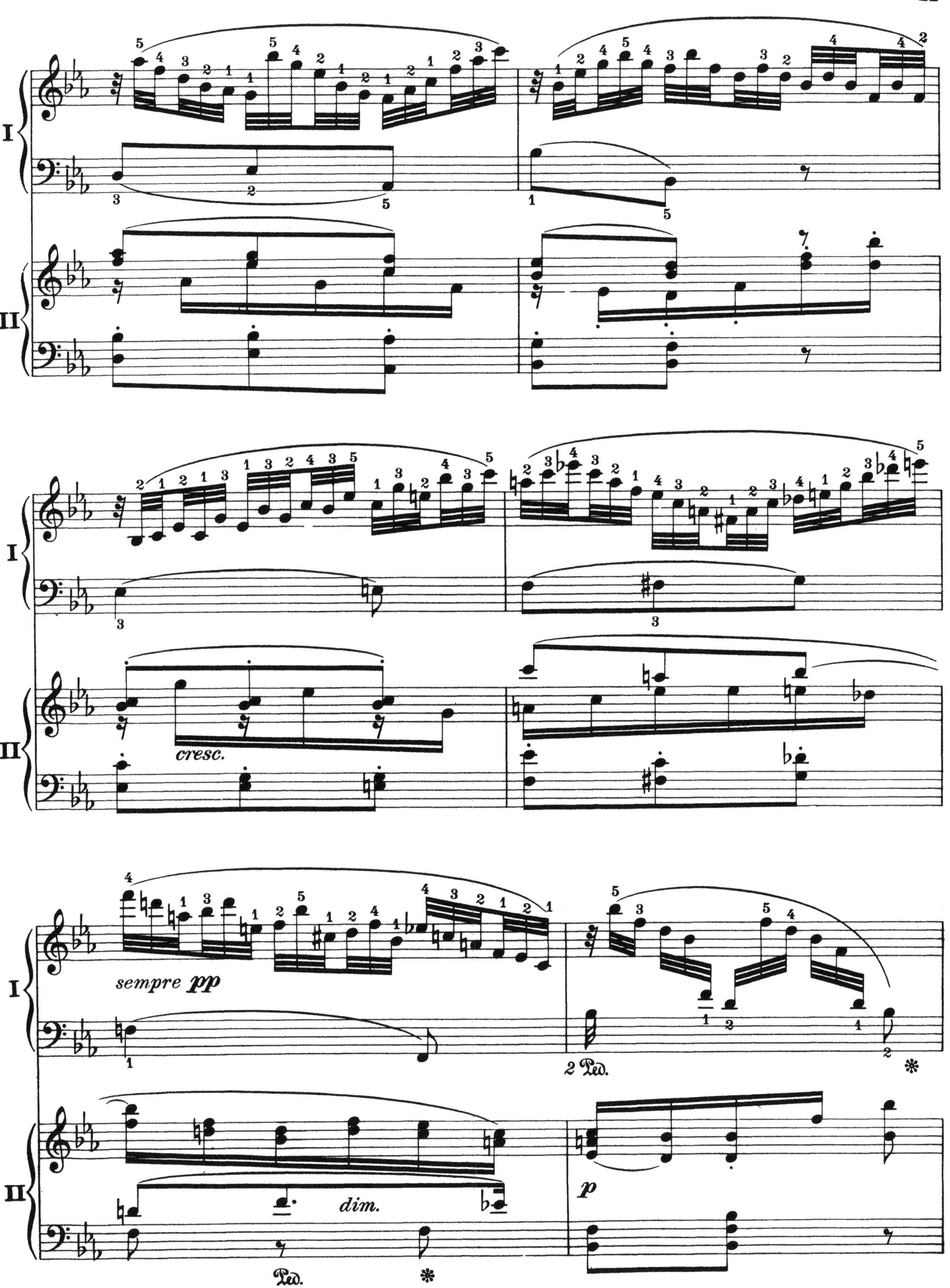
I
II
cresc.
sempre pp
2 Ped.
dim.
p
Ped.

I
II
p
pp
tr
D
Ped.
sf

I
II
Ped.
f
p
sf
mf
p cresc.
tr
E

I
II
mf
p cresc
f
Ped.
cedendo
p
pp
u.c. sin al fine

Allegro ♩. = 88
I
p
fiery and graceful
Allegro ♩. = 88
II
p
f
Ped.
p

II
f
Ped. ❊
sf
simile
ff

A
I
II
p
ten.
ten.

I
II
B
mf
Ped.

I
II
cresc.
mf
sempre cresc.
f
Ped. *
Ped. *

C
l.h.
I
II
p
mf
cresc.

I
II
p
f
Ped. *
Ped. *
Ped. *
I
II
p
I
p
I
II

I
II
Ped.
pp
D
p
simile

I
II
cresc.
cresc.
f
f
Cadenza
f
Ped.
42474

I
I
I
I
teneramente
p
I
II
p
pp
f

I
II
II
II
II
f
f
Ped. ✻
simile

II
p
E
f
I
II
f
p
I
II
I
I

I
II
I
I
II

I
II
F
Ped.

I
II
G
f
Ped.
42474

I
II
I
II
H
I
II
Ped.
Ped.
Ped.
Ped.

I
II
Ped.
p

J
I
II
pp
p
mf
f
Ped.

K
I
II
p
Ped.
cresc.

I
II
L
l.h.
f
p
Ped.

l.h.
I
II
mf
p
sempre cresc.
f
Ped.

I
II
mf
p
Ped.
Ped.

M
I
II
cresc.
fp

I
II
fp
fp
f
f
Ped.
Ped.
Ped.
simile
cresc.

N
Cadenza
I
II
ff
f
p
Ped.

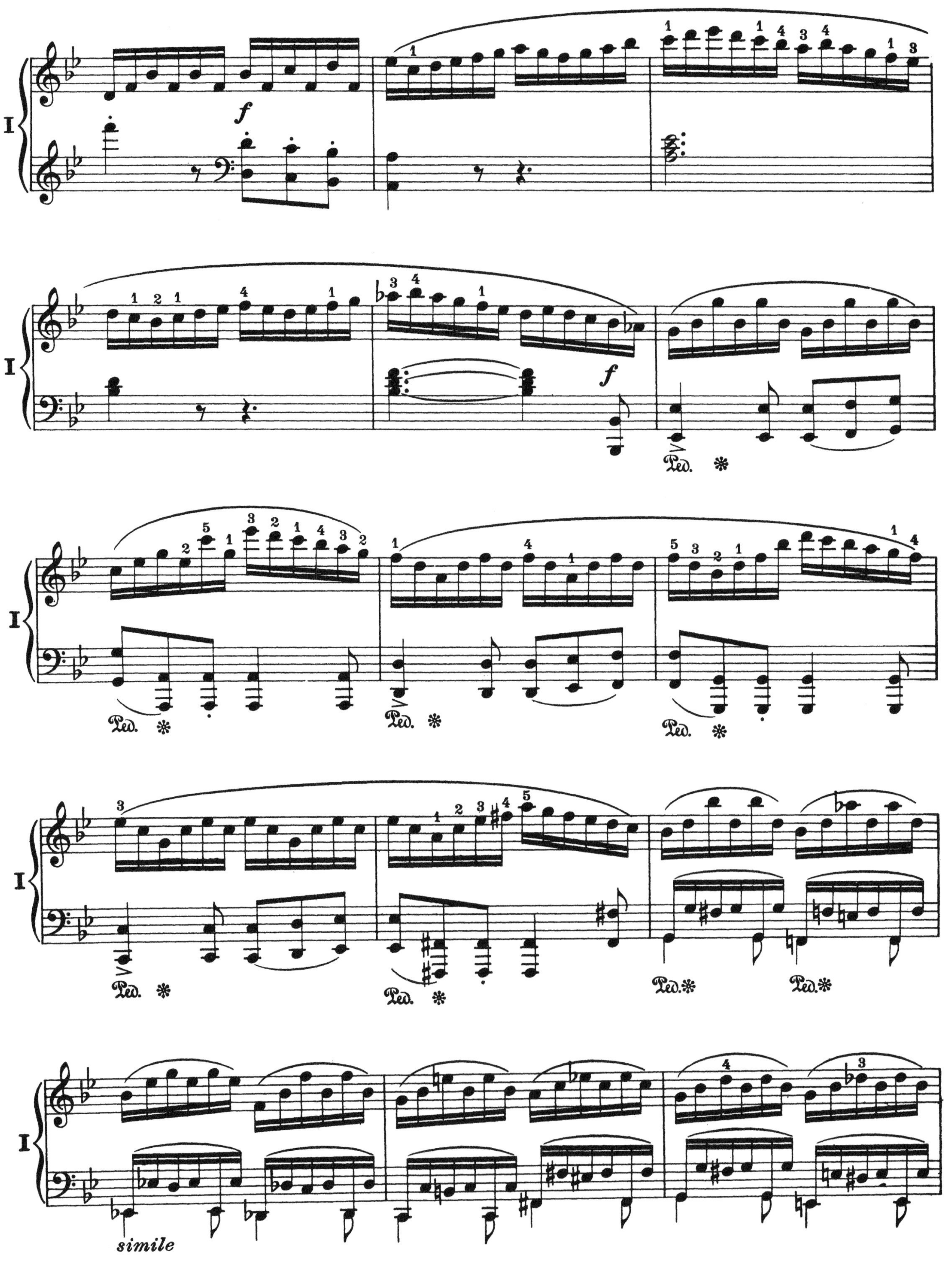
I
f
Ped.
simile

I
Ped.
tempo ritenuto
f
a tempo
p
II
a tempo
p

I
II
p
mf
Ped.
f
O
pp
sempre
cresc. poco a poco

I
II
sempre cresc.
sempre cresc.
ff
ff
Ped.